Pineal Gla

Ana

Review on how to descale, purify, detoxify, and activate the third eye

©2019, Evelyn Schneider-Mark

Published by Expertengruppe Verlag

The contents of this book have been written with great care. However, we cannot guarantee the accuracy, comprehensiveness and topicality of the subject matter. The contents of the book represent the personal experiences and opinions of the author. No legal responsibility or liability will be accepted for damages caused by counter-productive practices or errors of the reader. There is also no guarantee of success. The author, therefore, does not accept responsibility for lack of success, using the methods described in this book.

All information contained herein is purely for information purposes. It does not represent a recommendation or application of the methods mentioned within. This book does not purport to be complete, nor can the topicality and accuracy of the book be guaranteed. This book in no way replaces the competent recommendations of, or care given by a doctor. The author and publisher do not take responsibility for inconvenience or damages caused by use of the information contained herein.

Pineal Gland – A 360° Analysis

Review on how to descale, purify, detoxify, and activate the third eye

Published by Expertengruppe Verlag

TABLE OF CONTENTS

About the author 7
Preface 9
What is the pineal gland? 15
   History of the Pineal Gland 17
Material function of the pineal gland 23
   Sleep-Wake Rhythm 24
   Regeneration of Damaged Cells 26
   Aging Process 27
   Hallucinogen DMT 29
   Spiritual Function of the Pineal Gland 31
What is the third eye? 33
   The symbol of the third eye in various cultures 36
      India (Hinduism) 37
      Nepal (Buddhism) 39
      Ancient Egypt 40

- Middle East/Asia (Islam, Judaism, Christianity) 42
- Ancient Ecuador 44
- Children and the third eye 46

What impairs your pineal glands? 48
- Fluoride 49
- Other toxins 53
- Electronic smog 55
- Lack of sunlight 58
- Too little sleep 60

Activating the pineal gland / the third eye 62
- What changed for me after activation of the pineal gland 64
- Methods to activate your pineal glands 68
  - External factors 69
  - Internal factors 75
- Signs that your third eye is opening 77
  - Feeling the eye 78
  - Intuition 79

- Light Sensitivity 80
- The transformation 81
- Headaches 82
- Meditation, yoga and the third eye 83
  - The 7 Chakras 83
    - Root Chakra 86
    - Sacral Chakra 87
    - Solar Plexis Chakra 88
    - Heart Chakra 89
    - Throat Chakra 90
    - Third Eye Chakra 91
    - Crown Chakra 92
  - Strengthening of the third eye chakra 93
    - Stones 94
    - Aromas 95
    - Colours 96
    - Nutrition 97
  - Meditation and other activating exercises .. 98
    - Gaze upwards 99

The empty room	101
Visualising and feeling	102
Conclusion	106
Did you enjoy my book?	113
Book recommendations	115
List of references	121
Disclaimer	125

ABOUT THE AUTHOR

Evelyn Schneider-Mark lives with her husband Lutz in an old farmhouse in beautiful Rhineland, Germany.

Ever since she completed her studies to be a Naturopath and subsequently gained a degree in Psychology, over 30 years ago, she has been interested in marginal medical, psychological, spiritual and esoteric themes, which are often hidden from the main stream, but which are scientifically well accepted. She teaches this knowledge, not only to her students, but also reaches a wider audience in Germany with her various publications. In her books, she writes about subjects, the positive effects of which are widely unknown and on which she can pass on her own experiences. All of her publications, therefore, are based on indisputable scientific facts, but also encompass her own very personal experiences and knowledge. This way, the reader not only receives factual information about the subject but also a practical guide with a wide range of knowledge and useful tips, which are easy to understand and put into practice.

Evelyn Schneider-Mark's easy to read work puts the reader into a relaxed and pleasant ambience, while gaining insight into a subject which few know anything about but which everyone could profit from.

PREFACE

Is there really a relationship between the body and the soul? A question which has interested human beings for a long time. Recently, this subject has gained in importance. A tiny part of our brain, with the name pineal gland, has a big part to play in this. It is a very small organ, the function of which was long unproved, but one which plays an important role in our bodies, our spiritual life and our consciousness.

It can be seen from ancient writings that various peoples saw a connection between this part of our brains and the third eye. That begs the question: What is the third eye and what does this symbol have to do with our brains? A whole lot! You could say that this is the connecting point between our body and our soul. Our consciousness is embedded in this part. This is what this book is all about. I want to explain to you the meaning of this organ and your third eye.

What I can already reveal to you is that you also possess a third eye. In your childhood it was still open and active. It allowed you to have times full of fantasy and to see the world through your young eyes. Perhaps you even remember your imagination at that time, when wild fantasies felt real to you.

Why are we no longer able to see such things as adults? The explanation is to be found in this small organ in your brain. The pineal gland is very sensitive and reacts to external and also internal influences. But it is particularly the external influences which make it difficult to keep our pineal glands healthy today. They calcify and they become unable to carry out their function. Slowly, the third eye closes.

I thought to myself that there must be a way to open that third eye of our childhood once again. We already possess it and it is only waiting to spring back into action. Perhaps you are asking yourself what you need to do or how you can influence it? You are bringing the most important part of the answer with you – your interest in working on yourself to expand your consciousness and rediscover your third eye. The saying goes: Where there is a will, there is a way. I would like to show you the way and share with you my own experiences.

Firstly, I had to change a few things around in my life. I was not conscious of many of the influencing factors and I had never wasted any thoughts on them, I certainly had not seen them as damaging to my health. Did you know, for example that fluoride, which is to be found in many toothpastes and as an additive to salt, is pure poison for our bodies? That is only an example of things which made me think about making changes. After I had cleansed my body of damaging substances, I really started to feel better and more receptive to spirituality. It was like a purification of the body and soul which was already long overdue.

I will show you other things which are helpful in finding the connection with your third eye. Apart from pointing out the negative factors, which you should avoid, I can also recommend measures to stimulate your pineal gland and keep it healthy.

One perfect possibility is to be found in yoga or meditation. In our society, yoga has become very popular. Perhaps you also know some people who practise it. I, personally, find it a valuable balance for my body and soul which I could not imagine doing without.

Yoga has become popular. The teachings of the ancient Indians, however, are less known. I was unaware of these things too, at first. It was only when I started to become interested in the third eye that I realised that there was a lot I could do for my balance and enhancing my consciousness. I started to do meditation exercises which targeted the so-called 6th chakra, the location of the third eye. I practise these exercises regularly and they have become an integral part of my daily life.

With that as my starting point, I have found a way to develop myself spiritually. I have a much better knowledge of human nature, see many things clearer and I have become more sensitive to things which may happen. I rely increasingly on my inner voice, I trust it and follow it.

I would like to add that the information in this book offers a summary of the subject regarding my own experiences. I have deliberately kept explanations brief and simple for better understanding. Of course, you can go deeper and further into this subject if you want. I am just offering you a basis and practical exercises to start you off and to support you. After you have read this, you should be able to know how to optimize your daily life, how to decalcify your pineal gland and prevent further calcification.

I cannot promise that you will be able to expand your consciousness. You are the key to that. You alone are in the position to rekindle your third eye. It could take some time, or perhaps it will happen quickly. It will take the time it needs. Listen to your own gut and do not overtax yourself.

I hope, with my suggestions and exercises, I will be able to accompany and support you on your personal path. I wish you success!

WHAT IS THE PINEAL GLAND?

The pineal gland is also known under the following names: Epiphysis, Epiphysis cerebri or glandular pinealis.

It looks similar in its form to the cone of the Swiss stone pine. It is very small. In humans it is between 0.2 – 0.3 in. long and 0.1 – 0.2 in. wide, weighing about 0.004 oz. which is very small compared to a brain mass weighing about 45 oz. It is grey-red in colour.

This small gland lies in the middle of the brain on the back wall of the 3rd ventricle (Ventricles are hollow spaces in the brain which are filled with cerebral fluid) over the quadrigeminal plate. It mostly consists of pinealocytes and glial cells. Glial cells are nerve cells which support and isolate structures. The Glial cells increase in number quicker than the pinealocytes as the body ages, which causes the formation of cysts. These deposits of calcium and magnesium salts form so-called plaques which can be seen on X-ray pictures and have the medical name Acervulus (brain sand).

The pineal gland is already visible in embryos from the 36th day and is fully developed at birth.

HISTORY OF THE PINEAL GLAND

Research on the Epiphysis began in ancient times and has continued to this day. This gland had great significance in ancient history.

In the 4th Century BC, the Greek anatomist Herophilus of Alexandria described the pineal gland as "a sphincter which regulates the flow of thoughts". Even in those days, the link between the body and the soul was recognised. The Greek doctor, Galen (129 AD to 201 AD) described this particular organ as the "entry portal of the thoughts". The philosopher Rene Descartes (1596 to 1650) described the gland as the "seat of our soul". The ancient doctors, particularly anatomists, called it the "Corpus pineale" because of its appearance, similar to a pine cone. This is how the pineal gland got its name. Scientists are increasingly viewing our pineal glands as the biological third eye, the seat of the soul.

The Romans called the pineal gland "the supreme gland" and the Hypophysis the "subordinate gland". They described it as a gland a very long time ago. Modern scientists did not know that the pineal gland produces hormones until 1958, when they found that it represents the centre controlling the endocrine glands in the body.

In 1886, two scientists of Microanatomy – H. W. de Graff and E. Baldwin Spencer – discovered, independently from each other, that the pineal gland reacts to the fall of light on the retina, which is absorbed either by the nervous system or the outer eye. Perhaps it is no coincidence that the yogi texts of India and mystical traditions throughout the centuries speak of the "eye of intuition" and the "third eye" and point towards the pineal gland.

After this discovery, the two central hormones of the pineal gland were discovered: Serotonin and Melatonin. The next contribution to the pineal gland puzzle came from two employees of the National Institute of Health (USA), Acelrod and Weissbach. They discovered that Serotonin is the preliminary stage of Melatonin. They found out that Serotonin is made by a simple chemical process in the pineal gland.

In 1943, LSD-25 was discovered by Albert Hofmann by accident. This substance soon began to play a central role in brain research, because it was discovered that tiny amounts of LSD-25 could seriously change the state of consciousness. People spoke of deep religious and mystical experiences, up to paranoia and Schizophrenia. LSD-25 molecules are so similar to the structure of Serotonin that they can block the effect of the Serotonin in the brain. The LSD-25 molecules dock themselves onto the Serotonin receptors and take their places. To help you understand it better, it may help to imagine it like a lock and key. The two substances have such a similar key that both fit unto the same lock and can lock the door. In our case, the Serotonin has been locked out by the LSD-25.

At the University of Edinburgh, it was discovered that the changes in consciousness caused by LSD-25 happen because of this lock and key principle. LSD-25 deprives the brain of Serotonin. The change in Serotonin concentration in the brain changes the perception of normal reality greatly. This example shows that the Serotonin content in the brain is responsible for rational thought.

All these research results mean that our pineal gland is the organ which regulates the chemical composition in various states of consciousness.

An increasing number of brain researchers recognise that our identity is very closely linked to our state of our consciousness and that we are tied to our everyday consciousness. For example, Dr. Swami Karmananda Saraswati wrote in the Yoga Magazine Vol XVII No. 3, "It is clear that man is imprisoned in his mundane, everyday state of consciousness. He is locked up far more effectively than the prisoner who is incarcerated in chains or behind bars. Such a prisoner is only experiencing the imprisonment of his body, and he is very aware of his condition. However, the human being is far more effectively bound and tied. His very consciousness is held prisoner. It is so effectively harnessed that he cannot even perceive the possibility of higher awareness and experience. The ropes which prevent his perception of a reality in which he is infinite seem to be the levels of serotonin within his own brain tissues!"

MATERIAL FUNCTION OF THE PINEAL GLAND

The pine cone-shaped pineal gland is tiny but its size says nothing about its importance to our physical functions. This little gland is very important for our physical and spiritual processes. It is the control centre for our inner clock, regulates our sleep and wake function and increases our intuition. Once the function of the gland starts to slow down, the physical and psychological aging process begins. In the following pages, the material and psychological function of the pineal gland will be explained.

SLEEP-WAKE RHYTHM

During the day our bodies produce Serotonin and at night, when it is dark, Serotonin is changed into Melatonin. Both are hormones – so-called neurotransmitters. These act as connection centres in all nerve cells of the body, which send out, and forward on, electrical impulses.

As Serotonin influences our emotions, as well as many other processes, it is called the happy hormone. Apart from other things, it has a relaxing, strongly mood uplifting effect on our bodies.

Melatonin is the hormone that is responsible for our sleep-wake rhythm. The Melatonin production is dependent upon the amount of light falling on the retina of the eye. In the dark, where there is no more light, the production of Melatonin increases and makes it easier for us to fall asleep, while regulating the phases of our sleep.

The regulation of our sleep-wake phases is an important part of the circadian rhythm. The circadian rhythm is the ability of the body to regulate the sleep-wake phases into our 24-hour day, to help us to orientate ourselves on the time and enable us to carry out regular and repetitive processes, such as sleeping, eating and reproducing. It is also called the inner clock and is capable of re-setting itself to cope with seasonal changes and artificial time changes. These days we disturb our circadian rhythm by changing our geographical whereabouts, for example after a long-haul flight. Until our inner clocks have orientated themselves on the new time zone, we feel the effect as jet-lag. You may have noticed that at the beginning of a jet-lag phase, you may be very sensitive to daylight until you have got used to the new time zone.

REGENERATION OF DAMAGED CELLS

Apart from the regulation of the sleep-wake rhythm, Melatonin has another characteristic. It also possesses a strong antioxidative potential. It has the ability to reduce and destroy damaged cells. Studies have found that it has a much better effect than the synthetic antioxidant DMSO which is currently used in therapies. This product is known for its strong protection against electromagnetic rays, so the same probably applies to Melatonin.

AGING PROCESS

From the age of 17-20 years the production of Melatonin decreases dramatically. This effects the aging process, which is accelerated as a result. In addition, our susceptibility to sicknesses of all kinds increases.

There are scientists who believe that a reduction in the Melatonin level of the body is somehow connected to Alzheimer. There are positive test results showing the restoration and maintenance of the circadian rhythm, using light therapy and doses of Melatonin.

People report that they have noticed an increase in empathy due to taking Melatonin, which means that they are able to understand people's feelings better. This has a positive effect on their personal relationships. You should exercise caution when taking artificially produced Melatonin because the negative effects often outweigh the positive ones, like for example by causing an imbalance in the circadian rhythm.

HALLUCINOGEN DMT

The pineal gland produces a substance called Dimethyltryptamine, which is better known as its abbreviated name, DMT. This substance is also found in hallucinogenic plants, like Psychotria viridis and is known for its intoxicating effect. This substance is made into a decoction from the leaves of the plant and the psychedelic working drug Ayahuasca. This plant is well known in Brasil, Bolivia, Peru, in the Orinoco Delta of Venezuela, right up to the Pacific Coast of Columbia and Ecuador. The indigenous people of the Amazon Basin use Ayahuasca in rituals and religious ceremonies in order to attain an out-of-body experience. These people use it because they believe they can meet their ghosts and ancestors, see into the future or find healing for sicknesses and psychosocial conditions. Today, there is an Ayahuasca tourism in Peru. Many

Westerners travel to so-called "healing centres" in the hope of expanding their consciousness.

DMT is also known as the "spirit molecule" and is among the strongest known hallucinogenic neurotransmitters in our bodies. Rick Strassman researched that this molecule is dispersed into the body while in a meditative state or during a near-death experience.

Small amounts of DMT are dispersed, together with other molecules, while dreaming.

SPIRITUAL FUNCTION OF THE PINEAL GLAND

The pineal gland is the link between the spirit and reality. Our eyes recognise the material world around us and allow us to see the physical world. Our third eye – the pineal gland – recognises the spiritual world and allows us to see the ethereal world. In this way, we can react to events in the spiritual world and communicate with it. The world around us is recognised by our eyes, but the meaning and images of that world are controlled by our pineal gland. It creates our consciousness by giving our material impulses meaningfulness. However, in order for it to be able to do that, the pineal gland must be functioning smoothly. If the function of the pineal gland is restricted, the meaningfulness of the world around us is reduced, we see it as if through a fog. Because the strength of the pineal gland only slowly increases or decreases, we do not usually notice these changes. Over the years, we lose much of our spiritual strength, our consciousness and our imaginations, without even noticing it. If we are able to regain this power, our life would become much better and our joy in life would be restored. This is why we should work to strengthen and activate our pineal gland.

WHAT IS THE THIRD EYE?

The pineal gland is known as the third eye, as the seat of the soul or as the connection between the mind and the soul. If our third eye is open, we will be in a position to expand our consciousness. The desire to achieve sensitive perception is already within us, it just needs to be awoken. If we are able to do that, we should be able to acquire the following qualities:

- Strong intuition
- Good knowledge of human nature (e.g. recognising lies)
- Increased mental skills (e.g. concentration, memory, clarity)
- Strong ability to visualise
- Increased power of mind

- Extrasensory perception

In addition, the following spiritual areas will be activated with the open eye:

- Intuition
- Inner guidance
- Divine inspiration
- Presence
- Clarity
- Clairvoyance
- Imagination
- Telepathy

Almost all of these special phenomena can be scientifically confirmed. However, this will only be possible if the activity of the pineal gland is intact. We can only use all of these abilities if the pineal gland is active and negative outside influences can be avoided.

THE SYMBOL OF THE THIRD EYE IN VARIOUS CULTURES

Many cultures knew about the third eye, long before humans were able to confirm it in scientific study and had learned about the pineal gland. The symbol can be found in many cultures and always having a similar meaning.

INDIA (HINDUISM)

In the Riga Veda, the oldest part of the holy writings of Hinduism, you can see hints about the sun and holy spirits, which are described as the eye of heaven, an eye which reveals creation or an eye which never closes. This is probably where the well-known all-seeing eye originates. This symbol is a higher level of awakened consciousness which spiritual beings have developed and which humans can attain.

The Hindu god, Shiva, has three eyes. The third eye, known as the third eye chakra, is the eye of Shiva. I will explain the various chakras in a later chapter. The eye destroys everything when it opens. This makes it a symbol of knowledge which destroys evil and ignorance. This can be compared to the awakened higher spiritual part of a person, who sees the truth about things and destroys that which blocks out the soul of the person, in order to strengthen his divine consciousness. It is a kind of creative evil destroyer and an expansion of the higher consciousness.

Today, you can often find the eye of Shiva in jewellery designs meant to protect the wearer against evil and to give him wisdom and understanding both of the world and his life experience and to aid positive transformation.

In India, the third eye is symbolised by a red point on the forehead.

NEPAL (BUDDHISM)

Buddha is known as the Eye of the World in Buddhism. Typically, you find the eye of the Buddha represented on Nepalese temples. Statues of Buddha often show a point in the middle of the forehead depicting the third eye. These are known as the Eyes of Wisdom and Compassion.

ANCIENT EGYPT

Osiris is the Egyptian god of the afterlife, reincarnation and the Nile. The Egyptian hieroglyphics for this god depicted an eye, The Eye of Osiris.

Horus was one of the main gods from the ancient Egyptian mythology. Originally, he was the god of the heavens, a god of kings, a world or light god and protector of children. In ancient Egypt, the all-seeing eye was known as the Eye of Horus or Ra and was a part of the symbolism for Wadjet (an ancient Egyptian goddess of snakes). Various myths described it as the symbol of protection, healing and regeneration. The left eye of Horus was assigned to the moon and the right eye was assigned to the sun.

Perhaps the Eye of Horus was used to represent the part of our brain where the seat of our consciousness was to be found. It is interesting to note that in the depictions of the Eye of Horus, it is situated very close to the middle part of our brains where the Thalamus, pineal gland and the Hypophysis are to be found. It seems as if the Eye of Horus is a description of the Thalamus, near the eyeball with the eyebrow above it. The marking below could be the brainstem and the Hypothalamus. If these depictions were really meant to show that, it suggests that even the ancient Egyptians regarded the middle-brain as the centre of spiritual consciousness.

MIDDLE EAST/ASIA (ISLAM, JUDAISM, CHRISTIANITY)

In the Middle East, there is the all-seeing eye in the form of the hand-eye symbol. This is called Hamsa, Khamsa or Hamesh and is a further example of protection against the evil eye (bad luck caused by jealousy of others) and danger in general. It can also be seen as a lucky charm.

In Islam, the eye is linked to the Hand of Fatima. It is a kind of talisman and is seen as protective of and the most effective defensive mechanism against the Jinns and the evil eye. Neither the symbol, nor the alleged effect are really justified in Islam but are born of pre-Islamic popular beliefs which were adapted into Islam. The symbol in all its variations is often worn as a body painting, talisman or jewellery.

In Judaism you also see the Hand of Miriam which is often used as a talisman.

In a more Christian setting, you can see the symbol as an artwork called the Hamsa. It is called "the divine world", made by Khalil Gibran, a well-known Lebanese-Maronite-Catholic poet, painter, author, philosopher and theologist of the early 20th century.

In Greece and Turkey there is something similar to the Hamsa. Here it is called "Nazar" and is just the eye without the hand, but it is used the same way and has the same meaning as the Hamsa, namely to defend against evil. It is made into amulets or hanging ornaments made of blue glass.

ANCIENT ECUADOR

In La Mana in central Ecuador, an exciting discovery was made. It was an ancient artefact (this is the description given in the archaeological world for hand-made objects) called the "Black Pyramid" containing a total of 300 artefacts of unknown origin. It is also unknown from which culture they originate. The abundance of found objects is puzzling as they do not seem to have originated from that part of the world.

One artefact, for example, shows a king cobra with a hood from South-East Asia. The Black Pyramid is made of black stone with an eye at the tip. The stone is inlaid in gold, forming 13 levels which illuminate under black light. In total it appears like the Great Pyramid of Giza (7,500 miles away). The eye pyramid symbol is probably known to everyone, as it is known as the Great

Seal of America and is to be found on every dollar bill.

CHILDREN AND THE THIRD EYE

Dr. Swami Karmananda Saraswati said in the Yoga Magazine Vol XVII No. 3, March 1979:

"In fact, many children quite effortlessly possess many of the 'siddhis' or psychic powers associated with the awakening of ajna chakra. Children are often highly intuitive, can see into the future or know what their parents are thinking. They are uncanny in their ability to see the reality behind appearances- so much so that it is very difficult to deceive or lie to a child."

Do you remember your childhood and your perceptions at the time? Perhaps you remember the once or twice that you have perceived a situation which your parents or other adults around you have been unable to see, but which lived in your own world, impenetrable to others.

These characteristics occur in children because their well-functioning pineal glands are able to convert enough Serotonin to Melatonin. As we know, a sinking Serotonin level causes access to other consciousness stages. A reduction in Melatonin production is linked to an increase in the concentration of Serotonin in the brain, which in turn closes the door to the expansive world of intuitive awareness. Unfortunately, once this is closed, it remains closed to us for the rest of our lives.

The good news is that we are able to re-open this portal, if we pay attention to certain things.

WHAT IMPAIRS YOUR PINEAL GLANDS?

Our modern way of life allows our pineal gland to shrink and calcify. In the course of evolution, it has diminished appreciably. It has now shrunk from its original size of about 1.2 inces to only a few 0.2 inches. The reason for this is that we no longer follow our natural rhythm of life and we are affected by many disturbing factors and toxins. Many external factors with which we are confronted allow our pineal glands to calcify and eventually close our third eye.

FLUORIDE

The biggest enemy of the pineal gland is fluoride. This increases the calcification and reduces the activity of the pineal gland. We are often confronted with fluoride in our daily lives. We find it in toothpaste products, table salt or even, depending on the region where we live, also in drinking water. In German-speaking countries, such as Switzerland, Germany and Austria, it is not added to the water. In the USA drinking water is artificially enriched with fluoride.

What is fluoride? Fluoride was classified as a toxic agent until 1945 and it remains in our environment as a non-degradable poison. In 1936, the American Dental Association stated "At a concentration of one part per million, Fluoride is as poisonous as arsenic or lead".

What makes fluoride dangerous is that it collects in our bodies and leads to a slow toxification or calcification.

The amount that we ingest daily is incalculable because it is added to our table salt and so finds its way into almost every foodstuff. It is hard to find a product in the supermarket which is free from it.

A fairly new study from Dr. Jennifer Luke of the University of Surrey in England has officially confirmed that the functionality of the pineal gland is strongly inhibited by fluoride. The high calcification of the body, especially recognisable in the pineal gland, inhibits the spirituality of humans because fluoride slowly but surely disconnects us from our free will. In addition, it increases our willingness to accept and carry out the wishes of figures of authority without resistance. This was already used in 1945 to quieten prisoners of war in the German and Russian camps and make them submissive.

If you get into it more deeply, you notice quickly that it is a controversial subject. In the meantime, there are a large number of studies, including those relating to the intelligence of children, that show that strong intake of fluoride starts to show negative effects, very early in life, which are carried into our adulthood.

Previously, I was completely unaware of the dangers of fluoride. On the contrary, as it is always regarded as an indispensable product for healthy dental hygiene, I thought it was an important additive to toothpaste. I have now replaced it with a fluoride-free product, happily, there are very good ones on the market. My table salt no longer contains fluoride, I changed it when I changed my toothpaste. Luckily, we do not have to worry about fluoride in our drinking water in Germany, Austria or Switzerland. But if you life in the USA you might start thinking about alternatives to tap water, which is deliberately enriched with fluoride.

OTHER TOXINS

Apart from fluoride there are other toxins which have a negative influence on our pineal gland because they build up and harden the tissue, which then leads to calcification. These include hormones, quicksilver, aluminium, parabens, tobacco, alcohol, glutamate and refined sugar (household sugar). You can find aluminium in many deodorants, for example. Parabens are often used in cosmetics or as food additives. Glutamate is often used as a flavouring in foods, particularly in ready-made products.

Contrary to fluoride, I found the change to cosmetics and deodorants without paraben or aluminium much more difficult to achieve. My long beloved creams and body washes are unfortunately not as harmless for my health as I thought. I took a hard look at my products, one at a time and realised that I had to replace almost everything.

Fortunately, there are a few markets or shops which produce special cosmetics and deodorants which are free from these additives and which I felt comfortable with. I stopped eating convenience food, in order to avoid glutamates. Unfortunately, household sugar is found in many foods. If I bake and cook at home, I use more sugar alternatives, such as agave syrup or palm sugar, which also taste good.

Luckily, I already gave up smoking a long time ago. If you are a victim of this addiction, I suggest strongly that you try to stop because every day smokers take in incalculable amounts of harmful additives, apart from nicotine. I drink only a small amount of alcohol with friends but try to avoid it as well as I can.

ELECTRONIC SMOG

In 1879, Thomas Edison switched on the first lightbulb. It was seen as a breakthrough invention. Electricity continues to be crucial up to the present day. No-one could have predicted what effect this would have in the future. Now it is causing increasing problems to the environment in general and, not least of all, to our pineal glands.

What is electromagnetic radiation? Everyone using an electronically driven device, such as a laptop, WIFI, router, telephone or television, but also power lines, transmitters, cables and many other devices generate electronic and magnetic fields, these are invisible force fields. Today, it is difficult to imagine a world without electronic devices, which means that we live in a fog of electromagnetic waves and the radiation today is about 100 to 200 million times more intensive than 100 years ago.

All human cells communicate with each other using complex, low-frequency electromagnetic signals and biochemical reactions. This is how the information is transported which triggers the biochemical and physiological processes. The constant exposure of the body to electromagnetic radiation massively disrupts this communication. It causes abnormal metabolic processes which result in sicknesses.

Understanding these processes will help you to understand the effect electronic smog has on your pineal gland. Communication paths must remain unhindered to facilitate hormone regulation optimally. Often, disruptions cause sleeplessness or exhaustion because the Melatonin production or distribution is disturbed. In addition, because the pineal gland effects the Serotonin level it can also lead to depressions and depressive disorders. This all inhibits our spirituality in a big way.

How many electronic devices do you have in your living spaces? Unfortunately, they have become much too important in our lives, today. In my home, although I have reduced everything to a minimum, I am still subject to the WIFI waves from my neighbours. When I am walking out in the country, I leave my mobile phone at home. Before I go to bed, I switch the main switch off to at least reduce the amount of radiation. My mobile phone, which used to be my alarm clock, is switched off and outside my bedroom. I discovered that an analogue alarm clock does a perfect job in getting me to work on time. It is in any case worth asking yourself what electronic devices you possess, which are necessary and which are not doing much most of the year except sending out radiation.

LACK OF SUNLIGHT

We humans spend a lot less time in the natural sunlight as we did a few years ago. Our lifestyles make it difficult for us to get enough sunlight. Perhaps you work in a building where you only get a few minutes to go out into the fresh air, or not even that. We are surrounded by artificial light sources, which influence our metabolic processes, such as our pineal gland. Our four seasons have an effect on our hormone balance and our moods.

Studies have shown that in the winter months, our Serotonin levels are lower than in the months with more sunlight. This could be an explanation why the so-called winter depression occurs. It has a significant influence on our Melatonin production, which regulates our sleep-wake rhythm and our Serotonin level which ensures good spirits.

How often do you go for a walk? My answer to this question was that it was much too seldom. The more I went for a walk, the more I noticed that it did me good and so I started to walk more regularly. Particularly in the winter months, it was difficult for me to force myself. I was driving to work in the dark and driving home at night. Then I started using my lunch break to get out of the building and get some daylight. It is unbelievable what difference this little change made to my well-being.

TOO LITTLE SLEEP

Due to artificial light, night becomes day. Your pineal gland cannot rely on beginning its Melatonin production when the sun goes down because today, we switch on the light, so shortening our natural sleeping time.

There is a group of people who work nights as part of their job. This poses special challenges for our bodies. The body has to adjust its Melatonin production several times a month. You can determine whether your Melatonin level is not optimal if you are very light sensitive in the morning, after work. It is similar to jet lag. The body is in night mode and the sun dazzles our eyes. Once our Melatonin levels have regulated themselves to the new rhythm our sensitivity returns to normal.

When do you normally go to bed and how regular are your sleeping times? We often want to get a lot done during the day, making our day long and resting time shorter. I have to force myself to go to bed early and regularly. I try to read something before that, or to do something which has nothing to do with using a monitor.

ACTIVATING THE PINEAL GLAND / THE THIRD EYE

When people talk of opening the third eye or activating the pineal gland, they mostly mean the same thing. I think the same way, although for me the pineal gland as an organ plays a mainly external role, whereas the third eye pertains to more inner values.

The pineal gland can calcify, due to external influences, such as nutrition, environment and toxins, which can adversely affect its function. This has a direct influence on the inner eye, our ability to expand our consciousness diminishes. On the other hand, inner influences, such as faith or meditation can strengthen the inner eye. Activating the pineal gland, and the new consciousness resulting from it, have an impact on you. I would like to share my experience with you and show you which external influences you should avoid and which internal influences have a positive effect on your third eye, making an expansion of your consciousness possible.

WHAT CHANGED FOR ME AFTER ACTIVATION OF THE PINEAL GLAND

Be aware that the activation of your pineal gland and the opening of the third eye will result in changes, some of which you perhaps did not reckon with. Your new sense of awareness could overstrain you at first. As in sport, the pineal gland can have a sort of muscle pain after intensive activity with the third eye. This could take the form of a headache.

Start slowly and do not force it, because this can negatively affect the expansion of your consciousness. I had to deal with this at first when I began to activate my pineal gland. I wanted to open up my consciousness too quickly and I had to admit that I had started at too great a pace. When I recognised that, I started to work more slowly, take the pressure away and just concentrate on myself. I tried to be aware of my third eye without expectations.

The changes did not come with the magnitude that I had expected at the beginning. Things developed very slowly. I began to see everything more clearly and understand better. It is difficult to explain what I understand, exactly. It is much as if, when I watch something, it makes sense. For example, I had never paid specific attention to the buildings in my neighbourhood. Today, I pass the shops and other buildings with a clear vision and absorb everything. I used to pass by familiar objects without taking notice of them. When I look back, I seem to have been shrouded in a mist which had veiled my view.

I have become much more sensitive towards people. I recognise quicker when my friends resort to a white lie or want to hide something from me. Today, I do not always react towards people around me, I accept a white lie or when someone wants to avoid a subject. I see the reactions of my fellow beings much more clearly and give my friends more room to speak to me later about something or to console me with a white lie.

I can concentrate better and focus on things. I am less likely to be distracted and I am fully present. I see more clearly the things I am working on or which are occupying me and I remember events, in other words, my memory has improved.

I have strengthened my character. Today I am much more myself. I listen to my inner voice and follow it too. I allow myself to be inspired by other people, but I always go my own way. I was not able to do that before, I allowed myself to be persuaded without listening to myself, what I wanted or to recognise what was good for me.

I meditate regularly to keep these positive effects on my consciousness. In addition, I keep to the measures necessary to activate my pineal gland and to avoid calcification. I try to remain myself.

I want to reiterate that nothing will be gained using pressure. It is a long process during which you have to remain in contact with yourself and it could take a while before you notice the changes. But stay with it and give yourself the chance to open your inner eye and it will happen when you are ready.

METHODS TO ACTIVATE YOUR PINEAL GLANDS

Our pineal gland is a very small organ. External influences can exacerbate calcification which deposits on the gland, causing it to become impaired. In order to decalcify your pineal gland and to activate it, I have pulled the following points together, which I think will help you.

Try to integrate them into your everyday life and to live by them in order to maintain the function of your pineal gland over a long period of time. For you to open your third eye, it is essential that you watch out for, and avoid, certain external factors because only a healthy pineal gland is capable of opening your third eye to allow your spirituality to live.

EXTERNAL FACTORS

Firstly, we will concentrate on external influences to the pineal gland. In order to avoid negative effects, you may perhaps need to make changes to your everyday life. In the following passage, I will introduce you to a number of points which you will need to watch. Try to change these at your own speed and do not allow yourself to become stressed, it is supposed to make you feel better, not worse.

Detox your body regularly. For example, take mineral earth or healing clay with a strong binding capacity against toxins. You can get it in powder form or capsules. Green mineral clay Zeolite / Bentonite which is made from volcanic stone is particularly suitable. Similar to a sponge, the clay binds acids, heavy metals, bacterial toxins, fungal toxins, intestinal gas etc. and has a positive effect in preventing disorders and problems. Mineral clay has a unique structure and many indigenous people have been using it for hundreds of years in order to purify their bodies. Animals also instinctively use earth to clean themselves. The toxins bond with the earth and are excreted through the intestinal system.

Avoid use of fluoride as I mentioned before. Avoid fluoride foodstuffs, such as table salt, milk and tap water. In Switzerland, Germany and Austria, tap water can be used because it does not contain fluoride. In other countries, I recommend clarifying if the water contains fluoride, especially if you live in the USA. If in doubt, avoid it, for example, if you are on holiday. Change to fluoride-free toothpastes and mouthwashes. Replace table salt with rock salt or Himalayan salt.

Avoid other toxins in cosmetic products. Check to ensure your cosmetic products are free of parabens and aluminium. Aluminium can be found in many deodorants, today, because it inhibits perspiration, so reducing damp armpits and perspiration marks. There are, however, many deodorants which do not contain aluminium and are just as effective. You can find the relevant information on the packaging. Most aluminium-free deodorants declare that on the front of the packaging. You often find parabens in creams, lotions, make-up, lipsticks, aftershaves, deodorants, soaps, sun creams, hair-removal products and shampoos. They are used for their antimicrobial and preservative effects. In animal trials, certain parabens caused hormone-like effects. Warning: parabens can be found in the contents list under many names, such as Para-hydroxybenzoates (PHB), Oxybenzoates, Oxybenzoic acid, Hydroxybenzoic acid, Hydroxybenzoates, Metagin, Nipagin, Propagin.

Carry out bowel cleansing. This is an excellent way to get rid of as many toxins as possible to relieve the pressure on your liver and to ensure healthy intestinal flora. Chlorella algae are particularly good for this purpose. You can take it in tablet form over a period of 4 to 12 weeks. Existing deposits will be dissolved, harmful substances and heavy metals will be discharged from the body.

Drink 4 to 5 pt. of good spring water a day, so that a significant proportion of toxins are discharged out of the body through the kidneys.

Adapt your nutrition to cover more alkaline products. Use fresh foods and avoid additives, such as glutamate. Parabens can also be found in food because of their preservative effects. Avoid these products too. Try to stay away from household sugar and replace it with, for example, natural sugar substitutes, such as honey, agave syrup or palm sugar.

Try to reduce electromagnetic radiation. If you need to use WLAN during the day, at least switch off the router at night. Take your mobile phone out of the bedroom or keep it at least a few feet away from the bed. Ensure that electrical devices are kept to a minimum. Keep them out of the bedroom and if possible, the rest of your living area.

If possible, expose yourself to sunlight for at least 15 minutes per day, because sunlight activates the pineal gland and has a positive effect on your Serotonin and Melatonin levels. Your mood improves and it makes you more receptive to spirituality.

Try to maintain a regular sleeping rhythm. Go to bed at 10pm at the latest and avoid watching television and using your laptop or mobile phone.

Use essential oils to stimulate your pineal gland.
Try, for example, the inhalation of essential Neroli oil.

INTERNAL FACTORS

Now we have arrived at the internal influences that have to do with your attitude and your thoughts, but are just as important.

Sing as often as you can, the vibrations caused by singing stimulate the pineal gland.

Practice exploring the unknown and enjoying it.

Always try to put yourself in the place of others and try to understand their way of thinking.

Let go of right or wrong, black or white thinking.

Learn something new, it does not matter what.

Be artistically creative and enjoy being creative in everyday activities.

Think about your night experiences and dreams.

Collect experiences with spiritual subjects, not only intellectually but also existentially, with all your heart.

Practise overcoming emotional conditions, such as fear, guilt and feelings of purposelessness or worthlessness and avoid stress.

Meditation is an excellent opportunity to open your third eye. You will learn more about this in the following chapters.

SIGNS THAT YOUR THIRD EYE IS OPENING

When your third eye begins to open, your personality will change and you will improve your social interaction. In time, you will understand your place in the universe and see your existence from a completely new perspective. You will realise that we are the creators of our own reality. You will rely more and more on your own intuition and take steps to live up to your own potential.

FEELING THE EYE

Once your third eye is awoken and activated, it is possible that you will feel a dull pressure between your eyebrows. It may feel like a light touch or spreading warmth. It could happen out of nowhere, independent of whether you feel anything spiritual. It appears like a signal that draws you to your spiritual state of mind.

INTUITION

You begin to notice your intuition when you become mindful. This is probably the most obvious sign that your third eye is opening.

Intuition is the ability to recognise in advance that something could happen, or you have a feeling or sense that something is right or wrong. This comes and goes without prior notice. In time, this feeling will get stronger and will develop into a control process in your everyday life.

You may begin to feel or anticipate what your next action may be. Do not deny your intuition, but use this ability. It may not always be right, but it will certainly set you on the correct path.

LIGHT SENSITIVITY

The opening of your third eye can cause you to experience more sensitivity to light and it is possible that you will see colours more brightly. The colours seem to you to be more alive. If you concentrate deeply out of your third eye, as you would in meditation, it is possible that you may see the light of the third eye. Many people have spoken about this in traditional cultures, worldwide. It is to be found it many art forms and religious works. If you study them, you often see the light referenced in round or star-shaped forms.

THE TRANSFORMATION

The activation of a healthy third eye changes our perspective and personality throughout our lives. These can be positive changes, because you may have the strong wish to develop yourself further. Perhaps you see it in relation to how you treat others. Perhaps you have become more tolerant and less selfish.

HEADACHES

It is not particularly pleasant but despite that, headaches could be a sign for the opening of the third eye. The pain is stronger than that between the eyebrows. Accept it as an excess in energy and go into the fresh air or do things which make you feel better, such as meditating or running.

MEDITATION, YOGA AND THE THIRD EYE

THE 7 CHAKRAS

I would like to explain the 7 chakras in more detail, to show you the importance of the third eye as the energy centre. After that, I want to show you ways how you can activate your third eye through meditation. For this it is important to know the background of the 7 chakras.

The chakra system is exciting because it is written in Hindu religious texts dating back 3000 years. You can also find it in other cultures. Take, for example, the Incas, the Hopi and the Maya, who believed in a system of chakras which is slightly different from the doctrine of the Hindus but has basically the same meaning. In addition, it is to be found in specific forms of yoga, in neo-tantra and in alternative healing methods, such as Reiki.

In this country, the Indian system with 7 chakras is the best known, anchored by yoga philosophy. In order to understand fully the whole system, you need much more literature and time than you have available. Therefore, I want to give you only a summary of the individual chakras, so that you understand the build-up of your energy and how your mind and body interact. In this way, I can give you a further fundament to keep your mind and body in balance and activate your third eye.

According to the chakra teachings (and also Chinese Traditional Medicine) there are various energy streams in the human body, known as "Nadis". All these energy streams crossover mainly in seven areas of the body, which serve as energy centres. Each one of these energy centres is assigned to a particular characteristic, hormones, emotions, needs and body parts which can be simulated through these centres.

A particular function and sphere of life is associated with each chakra. Symbolically, you see the body of a human in the cross-legged position and the chakras are depicted from the lowest upwards. I would like to show you this order because one of them corresponds with the third eye. I will go into that one in greater detail later.

ROOT CHAKRA

The Root Chakra (Muladhara "support of the root") lies at the lower end of the spine between the anus und genitals, roughly one finger-width inside the body. Combined with the element earth, it is like the root of your body. It gives you courage, security and stability. If you are imbalanced, you will experience fear, nervousness and disquiet.

SACRAL CHAKRA

The Sacral – or, as it is known, the sexual chakra (Svadisthana, the "own home") – is affiliated to the element of water and can help you to adjust to changes, such as a healthy access to sexuality and creativity. Imbalance could cause shame, guilt or compulsive sexual behaviour. On the physical side, it can cause sickness of the sexual organs, kidneys and bladder problems.

SOLAR PLEXIS CHAKRA

The Solar Plexus chakra (Manipura "Area of gems") is situated in the lumbar region of the spine and radiates into the whole of the abdomen. This is why it is often called the inner sun. It is a significant reservoir for sun energy in the human body and stands for assertiveness, inner fire, passion and delight.

HEART CHAKRA

The Heart Chakra (Anahata, the "chakra of the silent note") lies in the heart area or the thoracic region of the spine. It is the centre of the 7 main chakras and represents a bridge between the three lower, physical oriented, and three upper, spiritual, chakras. A link between the physical and spiritual, between the body and the soul.

THROAT CHAKRA

The Throat Chakra (Vishuddha "centre or wheel of purity") lies in the cervical area of the spine and is the energy centre of the throat. It stands for bonding, openness, communication and expressiveness.

THIRD EYE CHAKRA

The Third Eye Chakra (Ajna, "command chakra") is also known as the Eyebrow chakra. Here, three of the most important energy paths flow together and join together into the Crown Chakra. It is attached to the pineal gland in the brain and is the seat of the soul. Intuitive knowledge and the highest insight are acquired through this chakra, the seat of primal power and the soul.

CROWN CHAKRA

The Crown Chakra (Sahasrara, "The opening of Brahman") lies above the crown and from there a "thousand petalled lotus" blossoms. According to Indian yoga tradition, this represents the final liberation from the circle of death and reincarnation. It identifies the space for its perception, which can never be the object of experience, but where everything appears the object of experience, even all the highs and lows of feelings and thoughts. When the advanced Yogi parts from his physical body at death, it breaks apart and the so-called Prana can escape.

STRENGTHENING OF THE THIRD EYE CHAKRA

The Third Eye Chakra is stimulated in many ways. Find out which is the best way for you. This does not mean that you must try everything, but if you are able to put into practice a few of these things in your everyday life, you will support your Third Eye Chakra, which will prove useful in opening your third eye. For me, it is mostly meditation exercises from which I draw the most strength in order to see through my third eye.

STONES

Stones can have a positive influence on your third eye chakra. Not least of these are the sapphire, the amethyst and the Iolite. My favourite stone is the amethyst, I particularly like its violet colour. I wear it as a necklace, mostly underneath my clothes as the UV-rays disturb its effect. I do not always wear it, only when I want to stimulate my chakra or during meditation. Pay attention to the individual recommendations of each stone, when and how it should be recharged or how it should be cleaned.

AROMAS

Particular aromas stimulate the third eye chakra too. Jasmine, incense, mint, lemon grass and violet can strengthen your chakra. Good aromas for burning include sandalwood, rosemary, peppermint, aloe wood, mastic, camphor, basil or juniper. I like to use joss sticks with these aromas. You can also buy special mixtures for strengthening the third eye chakra. I do not like to have the aroma constantly in my home. I prefer to take a break and ventilate the rooms in-between, then I can focus on the aroma again.

COLOURS

A different colour is assigned to each chakra. The third eye chakra is paired with violet and indigo blue. Surround yourself with the colour of the chakra, then what you look at will be nourished and alive. Particular colours have a big influence on your system. I like my home to be plain but I have added notes of violet with a cushion or a picture in the hall, so that my eye automatically absorbs the colour.

You can often wear violet or indigo blue clothes. The colours do not suit me very well, I prefer more subtle colours, so I use colours in other ways. Find out what you like best.

NUTRITION

It is recommended that you carry out targeted fasting to strengthen this chakra. St. John's Wort and teas made from elderberry, eyebright or melissa can support your fasting. Also berries, omega 3 fatty acid rich foods, dark chocolate and even caffeine are conducive to supporting this chakra.

I believe that a well-balanced diet with untreated, fresh foods is crucial to having a healthy body and soul. I try to avoid eating too much meat and try to obtain my foods directly from the farm where I am sure that no chemicals have been added to it. I particularly like melissa tea but I also occasionally drink St. John's Wort or elderberry tea.

MEDITATION AND OTHER ACTIVATING EXERCISES

There are various methods to stimulate or open the third eye. Meditation is what helps me to find and to earth myself. In this way I can better concentrate on opening and strengthening my inner eye. In the following pages, I will give you a few exercises to try.

GAZE UPWARDS

This exercise is from Kundalini Yoga. In this type of yoga, positions of the body or fingers and certain behaviour, including looking in various directions, are used to stimulate various chakras and areas of the body. The third eye chakra is linked with an upward gaze. It is a very simple exercise with an astonishing effect.

Take up your normal meditation position in a quiet place. You can do this exercise lying down or in bed. Close your eyes and gaze upwards towards the point between your eyebrows. Your eyes should not become tense. Relax.

Draw your attention towards your inner eye. Keep your gaze in the same direction. After a while, in deep relaxation, you may be able to see forms or colours. Perhaps you can see pictures which come and go instantly. Do not try to influence what you can see. Let everything come and go.

It is not a problem if you can only see black. Keep watching and relax as much as you can. The more you concentrate on the blackness, the more you will see structures inside it. It could be little spots, circles or a mixture of both. Whatever you see, the more often you do this exercise and find your inner eye, the more interesting it becomes.

You can also carry out this exercise during the day and with open eyes in order to stimulate your third eye. Do not overdo it. Exhaustion shows itself through headaches and pressure pains. Carry out this exercise only as long as it feels good and listen to what your body is telling you.

THE EMPTY ROOM

This is all about awareness of an empty room. This meditation is very effective to help you see with your third eye. You enhance your ability to "see things" and you learn how to use your new visual impressions.

Take up a normal meditation position and relax. Close your eyes and follow your breath. When you have become relaxed, open your eyes and look into the empty room in front of you. Let your eyes lie gently in their sockets and avoid any tension in your face muscles.

If you are practising this exercise in a room, you should not concentrate on the wall, but on the space between you and the wall. This exercise is especially suitable for looking into the sky or natural scenery.

VISUALISING AND FEELING

Visualising is when you trigger changes to body and soul through certain imaginary images. It is used mainly for self-healing and is a wonderful agent for decalcifying the pineal gland and opening the third eye.

The visualising and feeling technique can be used on the forehead, just above the middle of the eyebrows and on the pineal gland in the brain.

The Visualisation Technique

Take up a position where you feel comfortable. It does not matter if you do this exercise sitting or lying down.

Close your eyes and relax. Breath consciously in and out. Let all your everyday problems go. When you are peaceful and relaxed, shift your focus to your forehead or your pineal gland. Allow yourself time until you can feel this area clearly. Visualise into your chosen area a charge of bright energy in the form of a ball of light. Concentrate completely on this ball of light and feel your power. Recognise it with as many senses as you can and commit yourself completely to it.

It could happen, that a pressure builds in your head which becomes stronger and stronger. This pressure is caused by the mobilisation of energy, so you should not overdo it. End the exercise as soon as the pressure becomes uncomfortable or you feel tired.

Feeling the Pineal Gland

The advantage of the feeling technique is that you can always use it when you want to feel a specific area. Direct your attention to inside your head and feel the pineal gland inside your brain. Keep your attention on this so that you can feel it constantly.

You need not visualise or be particularly present- just feel with your normal consciousness.

The act of feeling and the light attention towards the pineal gland allows stimulation and releases energy.

CONCLUSION

We have been equipped with such a wonderful little organ in our brains and we should take care of it because its abilities are overwhelming. Who would have thought that our soul, our consciousness needed such little space in our brains? The interaction between the hormones and the neurotransmitters in the pineal gland is impressive, our natural rhythm is regulated by it and a natural regeneration process is always taking place.

Don't forget the effect of the DMT in the neurotransmitter, which can also play a role in our dreams and spiritual experiences, can help us to expand our consciousness. Our brains produce this strong hallucinogenic molecule naturally.

The symbol of the third eye is in no way a new phenomenon. The story starts long ago. Various cultures linked the symbol with the inner eye, the consciousness or soul. It always represents the connection between the man and the spirit. Today, this sign still has the same meaning and research continues to find ways of keeping the eye open or to open a closed eye. People often find themselves disengaged from themselves and not receptive to spirituality. Many express the wish to expand their consciousness and to find themselves again. The wonderful thing is that everyone possesses the ability to do that, even you.

Generally, I was shocked at how many sources are responsible for subjecting our pineal glands to toxins and poisons. It is evident that this sensitive organ is subject to many negative influences. I had no idea that hygiene products, like soap, shampoo, body lotion and also my deodorant contained many toxins that I was transporting into my body through my skin.

It was only when I had a closer look at these products that I noticed that I had to exchange almost all of them with natural products in order to avoid this happening. I also became aware, that I could dispense with many of these things, which I had been using for years, out of habit. Luckily, there are a great many alternative products which do not contain additives. Once I had got used to them, I found that they were just as good, if not better. It is definitely worth trying alternative products.

I always considered fluoride to be an important part of my oral hygiene and in the prevention of tooth decay. I never thought of it as a poison which left deposits in my body and had more negative than positive effects. I noticed amongst my family and friends that they were dismissive of my suggestion that fluoride could be harmful. People have the idea in their heads that is impossible to go without fluoride in the care of our teeth and that it could even cause damage not to use it, considering that the State adds it to table salt and drinking water.

Nevertheless, it is important for me to tell people around me what I know. Despite their scepticism, some people have mentioned being astonished after having looked into the subject on their own. It is hard to fathom why this substance is not discussed more, or even boycotted. It seems that people blindly trust what they have been told. Perhaps we are missing, exactly at that point, a clear view and need our expanded consciousness to recognise and react to the dangers of our world.

I am very grateful for the knowledge that I have gained to date. I feel as if my eyes have been opened to things with which I was confronted daily, but which I did not recognise. My consciousness has been strengthened to influence many things and I have obtained access to myself. I would never want to give up the clarity I have today. I feel closer to my fellow man and can empathise with him, which has also improved my relationships, generally. In general, I can trust my feelings in life more and that keeps me on the right path.

Looking forward, there are a few things that worry me. The technical development continues. Tests are being carried to provide more mobile network frequencies, the so-called 5G. More and stronger frequencies are being developed which, although they improve our connections, are incalculable risks for mankind. We can influence some factors which negatively influence our pineal gland, but we cannot escape electronic smog and are exposed to it 24/7. Therefore, it is even more important to get out into the countryside as often as possible where there is less electromagnetic radiation than in the towns.

I ask myself how the pineal gland develops in younger generations. Even small children are used to occupying themselves with the smart phones of their parents. I have seen this happening with children less than 3 years old, shortly before they go to bed. During this time the pineal gland is active and the third eye is open. Will calcification start earlier and the third eye already close in childhood through the use of smart phones at such an early age? It is a question which is not yet answered but it should give us pause to consider the issues with respect to our children.

The opening of the third eye should be seen as a long process. I hope that my book has helped to bring you closer to understanding how you can develop your spirituality and gain access to your inner eye. I am still working on mine. I wish you luck in finding the key to the door which opens your consciousness.

DID YOU ENJOY MY BOOK?

Now you have read my book, you know how best to reopen your third eye. This is why I am asking you now for a small favour. Customer reviews are an important part of every product offered by Amazon. It is the first thing that customers look at and, more often than not, is the main reason whether or not they decide to buy the product. Considering the endless number of products available at Amazon, this factor is becoming increasingly important.

If you liked my book, I would be more than grateful if you could leave your review by Amazon. How do you do that? Just click on the "Write a customer review"-button (as shown below), which you find on the Amazon product page of my book or your orders site:

Review this product

Share your thoughts with other customers

> Write a customer review

Please write a short note explaining what you liked most and what you found to be most important. It will not take longer than a few minutes, promise!

Be assured, I will read every review personally. It will help me a lot to improve my books and to tailor them to your wishes.

For this I say to you:

Thank you very much!

Yours

Evelyn

BOOK RECOMMENDATIONS

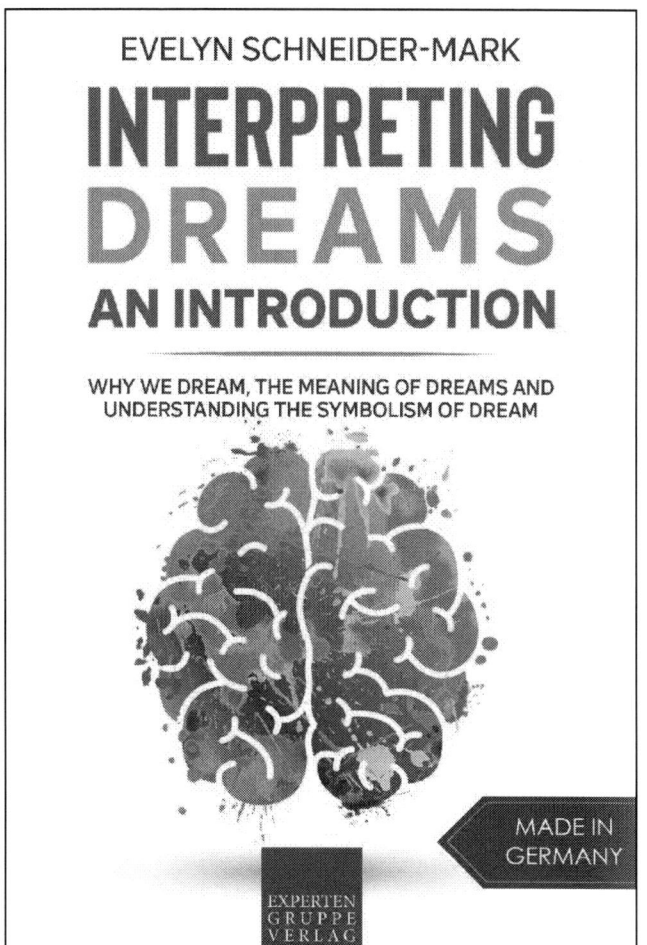

Interpreting Dreams – An Introduction

Why we dream, the meaning of dreams and understanding the symbolism of dream

Dreams have a high significance throughout many cultures which has not been lost over time. But why are dreams so fascinating?

Every night we dream for about 1.5 hours. During that time there is a fascinating interaction between our physical and mental processes which allows us to look into our mind and subconscious. Our heartrate can increase and we produce hormones. Scientists have not yet been able to tap into these processes so they have to rely on the memory report: the dream.

Interpreting our dreams is not an attempt to predict the future but is much more about understanding our subconscious processes and problems.

Would it not be wonderful if interpreting your dreams could help you to understand yourself better?

This handbook will not only help to give you the background knowledge you need but it will also explain why we dream and how to interpret your dream symbols.

Grab one of these books today and discover...

- *... what dreams really are ...*
- *... and how they can help you to understand yourself better.*

The Power of Breathing Techniques

Breathing Exercises for more Fitness, Health and Relaxation

We can survive for weeks without food and days without water, but only a few minutes without air.

Would it not be justified to presume that the air, which is more important for human survival than food or water, should live up to basic standards? How much air do we need for ideal breathing? And how should we breathe?

The amount of air that you breathe has the potential to change everything you believe about your body, your health and your performance.

In this book, you will discover the fundamental relationship between Oxygen and your body.

Increasing your Oxygen supply is not only healthy, it enables an increase in the intensity of your training and also reduces breathlessness. In short, you will notice an improvement in your health and more relaxation in your everyday life.

Look forward to reading a lot of background information, experience reports, step-by-step instructions and secret tips which are tailor-made to your breathing technique and help you to become fitter, healthier and more relaxed.

Sorbitol Intolerance

Living better with Sorbitol intolerance – background, tutorials, nutritional adjustment, recipes

Sorbitol intolerance is one of the least known food intolerances among many. And that, even though more and more people are suffering from it.

Wouldn't it be wonderful if you could at last find out if you suffer from Sorbitol intolerance? And how can you eat a diverse and delicious diet, despite your Sorbitol intolerance?

An increasing amount of industrially prepared food means that more and more people are taking doses of Sorbitol which they are not able to digest properly. This leads to a large number of lingering symptoms which are difficult to assign to any particular substance.

In this book you will find a simple guide on how to change your diet and a lot of important information about the subject of Sorbitol.

Read about fascinating background information, scientific findings, experience reports and secret tips which are tailor-made for you relating to your Sorbitol intolerance and which are designed to help you to achieve a healthy, longer and more fulfilling life.

LIST OF REFERENCES

Die Macht der Zirbeldrüse
From: Broers, Dieter
1st Edition, 2017

Werde übernatürlich: Wie gewöhnliche Menschen das Ungewöhnliche erreichen
From: Dispenza, Joe
1st Edition, 2017

Das dritte Auge: ein tibetanischer Lama erzählt sein Leben
From: Lobsang Rampa, Tuesday
1st Edition, 1957

Das dritte Auge: religionsdidaktische Anstöße
From: Halbfas, Hubertus
8th Edition, 2011

Theologie des dritten Auges: asiatische Spiritualität und christliche Theologie

From: Song, Choan-Seng
1st Edition, 1989

Die endokrinen Drüsen des Gehirns: Epyphyse und Hypophyse; ein Blick in ein interessantes Gebiet
From: Niehans, Paul
1st Edition, 1938

Anatomie: Zirbeldrüse - Regulation des Tag-Nacht-Rhythmus
Published in: Deutsche Heilpraktiker-Zeitschrift
01.12.2007

The Pineal Organ
From: Vollrath, Lutz
Publisher: Möllendorff, Wilhelm von
1981

Pineal Organ, Its Hormone Melatonin, and the Photoneuroendocrine System

From: Beck, F Brown, D Christ, B

01.01.1998

Die Funktion der Zirbeldrüse

Published in Philosophisches Jahrbuch

01.01.1913

https://www.zentrum-der-gesundheit.de/zirbeldruese-ia.html

https://krank.de/anatomie/zirbeldruese/

https://wiki.yoga-vidya.de/Chakra

https://slweb.org/luke-1997.html

https://www.zentrum-der-gesundheit.de/elektrosmog-ia.html#toc-elektrosmog-und-hormonstorungen

https://www.herzstueck-mag.de/was-ist-das-dritte-auge-und-wie-kann-ich-es-oeffnen/

https://www.asanayoga.de/blog/stirnchakra/

https://back2spirit.de/drittes-auge-oeffnen/

DISCLAIMER

©2019, Evelyn Schneider-Mark

1st Edition

All rights reserved. Reprinting, of all or part of this book, is not permitted. No part of this book may be reproduced or copied in any form or by any means without written permission from the author or publisher. Publisher: GbR, Martin Seidel und Corinna Krupp, Bachstraße 37, 53498 Bad Breisig, Germany, email: info@expertengruppeverlag.de, Cover photo: www.depositphoto.com. The information provided within this book is for general information purposes only. It does not represent any recommendation or application of the methods mentioned within. The information in this book does not purport to imply or guarantee its completeness, accuracy, or topicality. This book in no way replaces the competent recommendations of, or care given by, a doctor. The author and publisher do not assume and hereby disclaims any liability for damages or disruption caused by the use of the information given herein

Printed in Great Britain
by Amazon